This Is for the Brotha's a Biblical Guide to Understanding Women

By
Pastor Henry Owens Jr

Table Of Content

Dedication

I want to dedicate this book to my Lord and Savior, Jesus Christ, who called me, saved me, and gave me purpose. Without His grace and wisdom, none of this would have been possible.

To my wife, Latrice L. Owens, my lifelong partner in ministry and love—thank you for your constant encouragement, prayers, and steadfast support.

To my daughters, Tatiyanna L. Owens and Brittany M. Owens-Ellis, and to my seven granddaughters—Amiyah Jackson, Layanna Ellis, A'sani Ellis, Serenity Ellis, Grace Ellis, Zyiah Ellis, and Zariah Matthews—you bring joy and laughter to my life and remind me daily that legacy is born through love, faith, and family.

This book is also dedicated to every man seeking wisdom to love, honor, and understand the women God has placed in his life. May these pages help you grow in grace, humility, and strength as you pursue godly manhood and Christ-like relationships.

Acknowledgments

First, I thank my Lord and Savior, Jesus Christ, for the vision, insight, and anointing to complete this work.

To my loving wife, Latrice L. Owens, your unwavering faith and partnership make every calling possible. To my children, Tatiyanna and Brittany, and my granddaughters, your love fills my heart and fuels my purpose.

Special thanks to my spiritual parents, Pastors Glenn and Gwen Taylor of Reno, Nevada, whose mentorship and encouragement shaped my ministry walk. To Elder Waterford and Minister Bowers of Los Angeles, California, thank you for believing in my calling from my youth and helping me obtain my ministry license.

To my mother, Clester Willis-Jefferson, and my aunt Vester Moore, who inspired me to evangelize the world, and to my sisters Myrdle Broughton, Samantha Butler, and the late Patricia Owens, I honor your love and prayers.

To my brothers in life—Lenard and Monique Dotson; Matthew and Rhonda Knight; Anthony and Loretta Velasquez; Vincent Stewart; Glenn Taylor II; Eddie Butler; Mitchell and Geishula Moore Jr.; Terrell and Tara Taylor; and Tabu and Ebony McKnight—your friendship and faith have enriched my journey.

Finally, a heartfelt thank-you to Pastor Lenard Dotson, whose forward reminds every reader that brotherhood, love, and godly friendship still matter. Your words set the tone for this book's purpose—to help men understand, cherish, and honor women according to God's divine design.

About the Author

Pastor Henry Owens Jr. grew up in church as a child prodigy and was licensed to preach at just twelve years old. For over forty years, he has served in multiple church ministries and leadership roles, teaching and preaching the Gospel with passion, humor, and biblical depth.

A lifelong student of the Books of Daniel and Revelation, Pastor Owens is known for his revelatory teaching style that connects prophecy, practical wisdom, and spiritual growth. His ministry emphasizes biblical relationships, emotional healing, and the restoration of family order through Christ.

He currently teaches live YouTube and Facebook Bible study sessions each week, continuing to mentor believers worldwide. Together with his wife, Latrice L. Owens, he has served the body of Christ faithfully for more than thirty-five years, raising two daughters and rejoicing over seven granddaughters.

Pastor Owens's mission is simple yet profound: to help men become the spiritual leaders, husbands, and fathers God designed them to be—and to help them understand that women are not a mystery but a divine masterpiece.

Foreword

In 2008 I moved from Flint Michigan to Reno Nevada. That's right, Reno, Nevada! I moved to Reno because of a job promotion from the company I worked for. Shortly after my arrival I found a great church home in Greater Light Christian Center. It was there that I met Henry Owens. I often joke that Henry and I became friends because my first thought when meeting him was, "Something is wrong with this Brother!" This sparked our friendship since there was something wrong with me too! But I realized that what was wrong with us was actually right for the world!

As our relationship developed, our friendship grew stronger. I recall a particular incident that significantly impacted our bond. After completing a round of golf one day, while we were driving home, he spontaneously suggested, "Let us go and pick up a gift for our wives." "Pick up a gift for our wives?' I remember thinking about all the friends I've had in my life; I had never had a friend who made such a suggestion. In the midst of joking, clowning on each other and having fun this man paused to prioritize his wife. This experience that was entirely new to me.

In retrospect it is likely the small gestures of love like the one mentioned above and countless insights gained through years of successful marriage that have equipped Henry to author this book. In today's era of complex relationships and continually evolving societal norms, the importance of a husband and wife truly understanding one another remains paramount. This book takes its reader on a profound journey through Scripture, offering wisdom, guidance, and clarity on the nature of women, their roles, and how we can embrace a more meaningful understanding of them through a biblical perspective.

Throughout history women have been celebrated, misunderstood, empowered, and at times overlooked. The Bible provides foundational truths that illuminate their strength, purpose, value and significance. Whether you are seeking insight for marriage, friendship, or simply a deeper comprehension of the divine design of womanhood, this book will guide you with biblical principles rooted in love, respect, and wisdom.

I encourage you to engage with these pages with an open heart, an open mind, and a desire to learn. Do not merely read the content but compare it with your own thoughts and feelings. The ultimate objective should not be solely to acquire knowledge, but to be transformed by the insights gained. This book aims to serve as a source of reflection and revelation, enhancing your understanding of the women in your life and promoting a Christ-centered perspective in all relationships.

Pastor Lenard Dotson

Associate Pastor, Family Worship Center Church International, Flint Michigan

April 18, 2025

Synopsis

This Is For the Brotha: A Biblical Guide to Understanding Women is a transformational book written for every man seeking godly wisdom about relationships, communication, and emotional connection. With honesty, humor, and Scripture-based teaching, Pastor Henry Owens Jr. dismantles the myths surrounding womanhood and reveals God's true design for the partnership between men and women.

The book helps men rediscover what it means to lead with love, listen with empathy, and communicate with understanding. Each chapter draws upon biblical examples—from Abraham and Sarah to Boaz and Ruth—illustrating how God calls men to protect, cherish, and honor the women in their lives.

Readers will learn how women think, feel, and respond emotionally and spiritually; how to resolve conflict with grace; and how to build lasting intimacy through patience, prayer, and faith.

More than a manual, this is a ministry in print—a guide for husbands, fathers, brothers, and leaders who desire to reflect Christ in every relationship. The central message echoes throughout: when a man loves and understands a woman God's way, the entire family and community thrive.

This Is For The Brotha's

A Biblical Guide to Understanding Women

Introduction: The Search for Understanding

For centuries, men have asked the same question: How do I understand the women in my life? Whether it's a wife, daughter, mother, or sister, women often seem like a mystery—emotionally deep, relationally complex, and spiritually attuned in ways that can confuse the logical, solution-driven mindset of men.

But here's the truth: Women are not a mystery—they are a masterpiece. God created them with purpose, depth, and an innate ability to love, nurture, and inspire. Understanding a woman isn't about solving a puzzle; it's about appreciating a divine design.

The Bible provides clear wisdom about God's design for women. Genesis 1:27 tells us: "So God created man in His own image; in the image of God He created him; male and female He created them." From the beginning, men and women were created equally valuable but uniquely different.

This book is not a rulebook—it's a relationship guide, designed to help men build stronger marriages, healthier families, and deeper friendships with the women in their lives. Let's embark on this journey together.

Chapter 1:
God's Design for Women

God's Intentional Creation

Women are not an afterthought in creation—they are an essential part of God's divine design. From the very beginning, God crafted women with distinct qualities that reflect His nature. They were designed to be nurturers, encouragers, and connectors. These God-given attributes bring balance to relationships, families, and communities.

Proverbs 31:10-31 presents a beautiful portrait of a godly woman: strong, wise, compassionate, and God-fearing. However, this passage is not about perfection—it is about purpose. A woman's worth is not defined by societal expectations but by how she fulfills her God-given role in life. The Proverbs 31 woman is industrious, kind-hearted, and deeply rooted in faith. She uses her gifts not only to benefit herself but to uplift her family and those around her.

Throughout the Bible, we see that women play a crucial role in fulfilling God's plan. Women such as **Ruth, Esther, and Mary** were not merely bystanders; they were chosen to influence, protect, and lead in ways that shaped history. Their stories remind us that a woman's presence in a man's life is not a coincidence—it is a divine appointment.

A man who understands a woman's design will not try to change or suppress her; instead, he will appreciate and honor the strengths she brings into a relationship. He will see her not as competition but as a companion, created by God to walk alongside him.

What Men Need to Learn From This

Understanding a woman's purpose allows a man to lead with wisdom and respect. There are three critical lessons every man should embrace:

1. Women Are Multipliers

Whatever a man gives a woman, she will multiply. This principle is deeply embedded in a woman's nature. If you give her love, she will nurture and return it in abundance. If you give her security, she will create an environment of peace. If you invest in her, she will help build something greater than what was given to her.

This principle can be seen in many aspects of life. If a husband speaks words of affirmation and kindness to his wife, she will reflect that love and create a home filled with warmth and security. However, if a man gives his wife neglect, criticism, or anger, she will internalize it, and it will manifest in the atmosphere of the home. A woman's emotional and spiritual state is often a reflection of what she receives.

A wise man understands that his words, actions, and attitudes influence his home. He sows seeds of encouragement, and in return, he reaps a peaceful and fulfilling relationship. If he sows frustration, impatience, or disregard, he should not be surprised when his home lacks joy and tranquility.

Biblical Example: Abraham and Sarah

Abraham's relationship with Sarah illustrates the power of a woman's influence. When Sarah was encouraged and respected, she supported Abraham's vision and calling. However, when she felt insecure, such as when she encouraged Abraham to take Hagar, the consequences affected their entire household (*Genesis 16:1-5*). A woman will multiply what she is given—whether good or bad.

2. Women Carry Emotional and Spiritual Strength

One of the most misunderstood aspects of women is their emotional depth. A woman's emotions are not a weakness; they are a God-given strength that allows her to nurture, empathize, and connect deeply with others. While men often approach life with logic and solutions, women bring heart and intuition. These attributes are complementary, not contradictory.

A woman's emotional strength is evident in how she supports those around her. She has the capacity to love selflessly, endure hardships, and remain faithful even in adversity. Consider how many women in the Bible demonstrated resilience in times of crisis. Esther risked her life to save her people. Ruth remained steadfast in loyalty despite losing everything. Mary, the mother of Jesus, endured ridicule and suffering, yet she remained devoted to God's plan.

A woman's spiritual strength is equally profound. Women have an innate ability to intercede, pray, and seek wisdom in ways that profoundly affect their families. Many homes are held together by the prayers of a mother, wife, or grandmother. A man who disregards a woman's emotions and spiritual insight is missing out on one of God's greatest gifts.

Biblical Example: Hannah, the Mother of Samuel

Hannah was a woman of deep spiritual strength. Despite her barrenness, she cried out to God with unwavering faith (*1 Samuel 1:9-20*). Her prayers resulted in the birth of Samuel, one of the greatest prophets in Israel's history. A man who encourages and respects a woman's spiritual strength will experience the blessings that come from a woman who prays and seeks God's wisdom.

3. God Gave Men the Role of Leadership, Not Control

A godly man leads with love, not with dominance. Leadership is not about demanding authority; it is about serving with wisdom and humility. The Bible clearly outlines that a man is called to be the spiritual head of his household (*Ephesians 5:23*), but this leadership must reflect Christ's love for the Church.

Jesus led His disciples with humility, compassion, and sacrifice. He did not oppress them—He empowered them. Likewise, a man should not view leadership as an opportunity to control a woman but as a responsibility to guide, protect, and nurture her growth.

Unfortunately, many men misunderstand biblical leadership and turn it into oppression. They silence their wives instead of listening to them. They dismiss their emotions instead of valuing their wisdom. They demand submission without earning trust. This is not godly leadership—it is insecurity disguised as authority.

A man who leads as Christ leads will find that his wife naturally follows him—not out of obligation, but out of love and trust. A woman will submit to a man who loves her as Christ loves the Church—sacrificially, selflessly, and with deep respect.

Biblical Example: Boaz and Ruth

Boaz is a perfect example of godly leadership. He did not take advantage of Ruth's vulnerability; instead, he protected and honored her. He provided security without control and demonstrated integrity in his actions (*Ruth 2-4*). His leadership brought Ruth into a place of blessing, illustrating that true leadership uplifts and protects.

Final Thoughts

A wise man does not compete with a woman's strengths—he celebrates them. He understands that God designed women to complement, not to challenge, his role. A woman who is nurtured, respected, and led with love will flourish, and in return, she will multiply joy, peace, and prosperity in a man's life.

By embracing the biblical design of women, men can build stronger marriages, healthier families, and more fulfilling relationships. Understanding a woman's role in God's creation is not just beneficial—it is essential to walking in divine harmony.

As you move forward in this journey, ask yourself: *Am I leading with love? Am I honoring the strengths of the women in my life? Am I creating an environment where my wife, sister, or daughter can thrive?* When a man aligns himself with God's vision for women, he will witness the powerful impact that a godly woman can have in his life and household.

Chapter 2:
How Women Communicate

Communication is Key

One of the greatest challenges in relationships is communication. Men and women often approach communication with different intentions and expectations. While men tend to communicate for the purpose of exchanging information, women communicate to build connection and emotional intimacy. Understanding this fundamental difference is essential to improving communication in relationships.

The Bible provides timeless wisdom on communication. *James 1:19* states: *"Let every man be swift to hear, slow to speak, slow to wrath."* This verse serves as a guiding principle for how men should communicate with the women in their lives. By prioritizing listening, being thoughtful before responding, and exercising patience, a man can cultivate a deeper, more meaningful connection with a woman.

For many women, communication is not just about words—it is about being seen, heard, and valued. A woman desires to know that her thoughts, emotions, and experiences matter. When a man understands this, he can approach conversations with greater empathy and attentiveness, leading to stronger relationships.

How to Communicate Effectively with Women

The key to effective communication with women lies in active listening, emotional validation, and presence. Here are three core principles that can transform communication in relationships:

1. Listen Before Offering Solutions

One of the most common mistakes men make in communication is jumping to problem-solving mode. While men are often wired to seek solutions, women typically desire to be understood first. When a woman shares her thoughts or concerns, she is not necessarily looking for an immediate fix—she is seeking a listening ear and emotional connection.

When a woman expresses frustration or sadness, a man's first instinct might be to offer advice or suggest a solution. However, this can make a woman feel as though her emotions are being dismissed. Instead of rushing to fix the issue, a man should take the time to listen and acknowledge her feelings.

Example: If a woman comes home from work and says, *"Today was so stressful. My boss was being unfair,"* instead of responding with *"Just talk to your boss and set boundaries,"* a better response would be *"That sounds really frustrating. Tell me more about what happened."* By doing this, a man validates her experience and fosters emotional intimacy.

A good listener pays attention not just to words but to tone, body language, and emotions. He asks open-ended questions, nods in agreement, and provides affirmations such as *"I hear you"* or *"That makes sense."* When a woman feels truly heard, she feels loved.

2. Validate Her Feelings

Validation is a crucial component of effective communication. Women want to feel that their emotions are acknowledged and respected. Too often, men unintentionally invalidate a woman's feelings by dismissing or minimizing them.

Saying *"You're overreacting"* or *"It's not that big of a deal"* can make a woman feel unheard and unimportant. Instead, statements such as *"I understand why that upset you"* or *"That sounds really difficult"* create a safe space for her to express herself without judgment.

Example: If a woman is upset about an argument with a friend and says, *"I can't believe she said that to me. It really hurt,"* an invalidating response would be, *"Just forget about it. It's not worth being upset over."* A validating response would be, *"I can see why that hurt. It's tough when someone you trust says something like that."* This type of response reassures a woman that her feelings are important and that she has the right to express them.

Validation does not mean agreeing with everything a woman says, but it does mean acknowledging her emotions and showing empathy. When a woman feels that her emotions are respected, she is more likely to feel secure and appreciated in the relationship.

3. Be Present

In today's fast-paced world, distractions are everywhere. Whether it's work, social media, or other obligations, it's easy to become mentally absent even when physically present. However, when it comes to communication, **presence is one of the most valuable gifts a man can give to a woman.**

Quality time and active engagement are essential in making a woman feel valued. A few moments of focused attention are more meaningful than hours of distracted interaction. Simple gestures such as putting away the phone, maintaining eye contact, and truly listening during conversations can make a significant difference.

Example: If a woman starts talking about her day and notices that her partner is scrolling on his phone or responding with half-hearted *"uh-huhs,"* she will likely feel unimportant. However, if he sets the phone aside, looks into her eyes, and engages with her words, she will feel cherished and appreciated.

Being present also means engaging in meaningful conversations beyond surface-level topics. Instead of only discussing tasks, responsibilities, or logistical matters, a man should make an effort to talk about emotions, dreams, and deeper subjects that build emotional intimacy.

Why This Matters

When a woman feels heard, she feels loved. Communication is the foundation of any strong relationship, and learning to communicate effectively with a woman fosters trust, emotional connection, and harmony.

A man who actively listens, validates a woman's emotions, and remains fully present in conversations will see a positive shift in his relationships. Women are naturally drawn to emotional depth, and when a man takes the time to communicate with patience and empathy, he creates an environment where love and respect flourish.

By applying these principles, men can strengthen their relationships, avoid unnecessary conflicts, and build a deeper bond with the women in their lives. Communication is not just about talking—it is about understanding, affirming, and connecting.

Let every man take to heart the wisdom of *James 1:19*—*"Let every man be swift to hear, slow to speak, slow to wrath."* By listening first, choosing words wisely, and showing patience, men can become better communicators, better partners, and better leaders in their homes and communities.

Chapter 3:
A Woman's Emotional Needs

Understanding a Woman's Heart

A woman doesn't just want to be loved—she wants to be cherished. She desires security, consistency, and emotional connection. Love alone is not enough; she needs to know that she is valued, appreciated, and deeply connected to her partner emotionally and spiritually.

Ephesians 5:25 provides clear guidance on how a man should love a woman: *"Husbands, love your wives, just as Christ also loved the church and gave Himself for her."* This verse highlights sacrificial, selfless love—one that prioritizes her well-being, security, and growth above all else. Just as Christ nurtures and protects His church, a man must nurture and protect the heart of the woman in his life.

A woman who feels cherished thrives in every aspect of her life. When a man provides her with emotional security and validates her feelings, she reciprocates with love, support, and encouragement. Understanding and meeting a woman's emotional needs is one of the greatest responsibilities of a man in a relationship.

The Five Core Emotional Needs of Women

Every woman has five core emotional needs. When these needs are met, she flourishes in her relationships, her home, and her faith. These five needs are:

1. Love and Affection (Song of Solomon 1:2)

Women need consistent expressions of love, not just in words but in actions. Love should not be something that is assumed; it should be demonstrated daily through small gestures, kind words, and meaningful acts of service.

Song of Solomon 1:2 beautifully expresses a woman's desire for affection: *"Let him kiss me with the kisses of his mouth—for your love is more delightful than wine."* This passage reflects the power of love and its deep emotional impact.

Affection is more than just physical touch—it includes thoughtful compliments, reassuring words, and expressions of appreciation. A woman needs to feel adored and pursued, not just during the early stages of a relationship but throughout her life. Simple gestures such as holding her hand, leaving a thoughtful note, or expressing appreciation go a long way in fulfilling her need for love and affection.

2. Emotional Security (Proverbs 31:11)

A woman thrives when she feels safe—physically, emotionally, and spiritually. *Proverbs 31:11* states: *"Her husband has full confidence in her and lacks nothing of value."* This verse emphasizes the importance of trust and security in a relationship.

Emotional security means that a woman can trust that her partner will be there for her through the ups and downs of life. It means knowing that her emotions will be respected, her concerns will be heard, and her well-being will always be a priority.

When a man provides emotional security, a woman does not feel the need to suppress her feelings or fear rejection. Instead, she opens up, knowing that her thoughts and emotions matter. A man who creates a safe space for a woman fosters deep trust and a stronger emotional bond.

3. Meaningful Conversation (1 Peter 3:7)

Communication is about more than just exchanging words—it is about building connection. Women long for meaningful conversations that go beyond the surface, conversations that allow them to share their thoughts, emotions, and dreams.

1 Peter 3:7 instructs men: *"Husbands, likewise, dwell with them with understanding, giving honor to the wife, as to the weaker vessel, and as being heirs together of the grace of life, that your prayers may not be hindered."* This verse highlights the need for understanding and communication within a relationship.

Meaningful conversation requires active listening, genuine interest, and emotional engagement. It is not just about responding to what she says, but about seeking to understand her perspective, feelings, and desires. A woman feels deeply connected to a man who takes the time to engage in thoughtful discussions, listen attentively, and express his thoughts openly.

Instead of only discussing responsibilities and daily tasks, a man should make an effort to have deeper conversations with his partner. Talking about emotions, dreams, faith, and personal experiences strengthens the emotional connection between them.

4. Spiritual Leadership (Ephesians 5:23)

A godly man sets the spiritual tone for his home. Ephesians 5:23 states: "For the husband is the head of the wife, as Christ is the head of the church, his body, of which he is the Savior." This verse calls men to lead with wisdom, humility, and faith.

Spiritual leadership does not mean controlling or dictating—it means guiding, praying, and setting an example of faithfulness. A woman finds great security in a man who prioritizes his relationship with God and encourages her to do the same.

When a man prays for his wife, leads his family in devotion, and seeks God's wisdom, he strengthens the spiritual foundation of their relationship. Women deeply appreciate men who take responsibility for the spiritual health of the household. A woman who feels spiritually supported is more likely to grow in her faith and trust her husband's leadership.

5. Appreciation and Honor (Proverbs 31:28)

Women flourish when they feel valued. *Proverbs 31:28* describes the impact of appreciation: *"Her children arise and call her blessed; her husband also, and he praises her."* A woman who is honored and appreciated will give her best in return.

Appreciation is not just about acknowledging what a woman does—it is about recognizing who she is. Too often, women go unnoticed for their contributions, whether in the home, workplace, or ministry. A man should never take for granted the efforts, sacrifices, and love that a woman gives so freely.

Simple words of affirmation, acts of gratitude, and recognition of her strengths make a profound impact. A husband who praises his wife, acknowledges her hard work, and celebrates her uniqueness strengthens her confidence and emotional well-being.

When a woman feels honored, she responds with love, joy, and unwavering support. A man who takes the time to appreciate the woman in his life builds a foundation of mutual respect and admiration.

Final Thoughts

A woman's emotional needs are not complicated, but they do require intentional effort. Love, security, communication, spiritual leadership, and appreciation are the keys to making a woman feel cherished and valued.

When a man commits to meeting these emotional needs, he fosters a relationship that is built on trust, understanding, and deep emotional intimacy. The wisdom found in *Ephesians 5:25, Proverbs 31, Song of Solomon, and 1 Peter 3:7* serves as a guide for men who desire to love their wives as Christ loves the church.

If a man strives to provide love, security, meaningful conversations, spiritual leadership, and appreciation, he will see his relationship flourish. Women are designed by God to love deeply, and when they receive the emotional support they need, they will naturally multiply that love back into the relationship.

A man who understands and honors a woman's emotional needs is not just fulfilling his role—he is cultivating a love that reflects God's perfect design.

Chapter 4:
Understanding a Woman's Sexuality and Intimacy Needs

1 Corinthians 7:3-5 – Marriage is About Mutual Giving

Intimacy in marriage is not merely a physical act—it is an emotional, spiritual, and relational bond that reflects God's design for love and unity. *1 Corinthians 7:3-5* states: *"The husband should fulfill his marital duty to his wife, and likewise the wife to her husband. The wife does not have authority over her own body but yields it to her husband. In the same way, the husband does not have authority over his own body but yields it to his wife."* This passage highlights the mutual nature of intimacy in marriage.

For many women, physical intimacy is deeply tied to emotional security. A woman must first feel emotionally connected before she can fully engage in physical intimacy. When a husband prioritizes emotional connection, he creates an environment where intimacy is a natural and fulfilling part of the relationship.

Mutual love, respect, and sacrifice are the cornerstones of intimacy. A man must approach intimacy with emotional sensitivity, understanding that a woman's heart must be nurtured long before any physical interaction takes place. He should invest in her emotionally and spiritually so that their physical connection is a reflection of the deep love and unity they share.

Emotional Connection is the Foundation of Physical Intimacy

A woman's desire for physical intimacy is often rooted in how secure she feels in her relationship. Emotional intimacy and physical intimacy are intertwined—without emotional closeness, physical intimacy can feel empty or even burdensome. A husband must invest in his wife's heart consistently, ensuring that she feels safe, loved, and cherished.

Ways to Cultivate Emotional Connection:

1. **Engage in Thoughtful Conversations** – Take time to ask how she feels, what her day was like, and what is on her heart.

2. **Practice Active Listening** – Show genuine interest in her emotions and experiences without dismissing or rushing to fix her concerns.

3. **Spend Quality Time Together** – Set aside time for date nights, meaningful moments, and shared activities.

4. **Show Consistency** – Emotional connection cannot be sporadic; it requires daily effort and intentionality.

When a husband invests in these small, meaningful actions, his wife will feel emotionally secure. This security opens the door for greater physical intimacy because she knows she is valued beyond just physical attraction.

The Difference Between Physical Attraction and Emotional Intimacy

There is a significant difference between being physically attracted to someone and being intimately connected on a deeper level. Physical attraction is often immediate and external, but true intimacy is built over time and requires trust, emotional investment, and spiritual unity.

Key Differences:

- **Physical Attraction:** Based on appearance, chemistry, and external qualities.
- **Emotional Intimacy:** Built on trust, shared experiences, deep conversations, and mutual support.

While physical attraction may bring two people together, it is emotional intimacy that sustains a long-term, fulfilling relationship. A man who only focuses on the physical aspect of intimacy without nurturing emotional closeness will eventually create distance in his marriage.

How to Cultivate Emotional Intimacy in Marriage:

1. **Prioritize Non-Physical Forms of Affection** – Holding hands, hugging, and small gestures of affection outside the bedroom reinforce emotional closeness.
2. **Speak Her Love Language** – Whether it's words of affirmation, acts of service, quality time, or gifts, expressing love in her preferred way strengthens the bond between husband and wife.
3. **Encourage Vulnerability** – Create a safe space where she feels comfortable expressing her fears, dreams, and emotions without judgment.
4. **Be Present in Everyday Moments** – Simple acts of kindness, laughter, and shared experiences build intimacy over time.

When a woman feels emotionally cherished, she will naturally be more open to physical intimacy. The deeper the emotional bond, the stronger the physical connection will be.

Creating an Atmosphere Where a Woman Feels Cherished, Not Just Desired

A woman does not want to feel like an object of desire—she wants to feel cherished for who she is as a person, not just for what she can offer physically. Many women struggle with intimacy when they feel that their worth is only tied to their physical appearance or what they provide in the bedroom. True intimacy comes when a husband makes his wife feel loved, valued, and irreplaceable.

How to Make a Woman Feel Cherished:

- **Show Appreciation for Who She Is** – Compliment her character, intelligence, and kindness, not just her physical attributes.
- **Be Gentle and Patient** – Rushing intimacy without considering her emotions can create distance.
- **Make Her Feel Secure** – When a woman knows she is the only one in your heart and mind, she will naturally feel more connected.
- **Initiate Non-Sexual Affection** – Holding her hand, cuddling, and expressing love in non-physical ways strengthen intimacy.

A husband who focuses on his wife's emotional and spiritual well-being creates an environment where intimacy flourishes. He does not see intimacy as something to take but as something to give—a reflection of the deep love and unity they share.

Final Thoughts

Understanding a woman's sexuality and intimacy needs requires patience, love, and a commitment to emotional connection. A fulfilling intimate relationship is built on the principles of *1 Corinthians 7:3-5*, where both husband and wife honor each other's needs and prioritize giving over taking.

When a man prioritizes emotional intimacy, physical intimacy becomes a natural extension of their bond. Love, respect, and sacrifice create an environment where a woman feels safe, cherished, and eager to express her love fully. By cultivating emotional connection, valuing trust over mere attraction, and making a woman feel truly cherished, a husband strengthens the foundation of intimacy in his marriage.

Marriage is not just about fulfilling physical needs—it is about building a deep, unbreakable connection that reflects God's love and design for relationships. A man who understands and honors his wife's needs will experience a relationship filled with love, passion, and unwavering commitment.

Chapter 5:
The Power of a Woman's Influence

Proverbs 14:1 – "A Wise Woman Builds Her House"

Women have a profound impact on the atmosphere of their home and family. *Proverbs 14:1* states: *"A wise woman builds her house, but a foolish one tears it down with her own hands."* This scripture reveals the incredible responsibility and power a woman holds within her household. Her words, actions, and spirit shape the emotional and spiritual climate in ways that influence every member of her family.

A woman who is loved, cherished, and supported by her husband will naturally cultivate an environment of peace, joy, and encouragement. When a man fosters love and respect in his home, his wife will multiply that love and create a nurturing space for their family to thrive.

However, when a man neglects his role as an emotional and spiritual leader, frustration can take root, leading to tension, disconnect, and disharmony in the household. A woman who feels unappreciated or unsupported may struggle to pour into her family in the way that God designed. A wise man understands that his treatment of his wife directly affects the atmosphere of his home.

How Women Shape the Home, Family, and Spiritual Climate

A woman's influence is far-reaching—her presence and actions leave a lasting imprint on her husband, children, and community.

She sets the tone of the home through her words, behavior, and faith. A woman's ability to encourage, nurture, and guide is a divine gift that strengthens the foundation of her family.

1. A Woman's Words Shape the Household

The words spoken in a home can either build up or tear down. Encouraging, faith-filled words spoken by a wife and mother create an environment where love flourishes. Conversely, constant criticism, negativity, or harsh words can sow seeds of doubt, insecurity, and division.

Proverbs 31:26 says: *"She speaks with wisdom, and faithful instruction is on her tongue."* A woman who speaks life into her family strengthens their confidence, uplifts their spirits, and reinforces a culture of faith and trust.

2. A Woman's Actions Influence Her Family's Growth

Beyond words, a woman's daily actions play a crucial role in the health of her home. She demonstrates love through her service, selflessness, and commitment to those she cares for. Her willingness to lead in kindness and patience sets an example for her children and inspires her husband.

A nurturing wife teaches her family how to handle challenges with grace. She leads by example, showing her children the importance of integrity, hard work, and faith in God's plan. Her presence is a stabilizing force, bringing comfort and security to those around her.

3. A Woman's Faith Shapes the Spiritual Climate

A woman's relationship with God has a significant effect on the spiritual strength of her family. Many homes are covered in prayer because of a faithful wife or mother who intercedes on behalf of her loved ones.

Consider the example of Hannah in *1 Samuel 1:10-20*—her fervent prayers led to the birth of Samuel, a great prophet of Israel. A woman who prays for her family, encourages faith, and fosters a home filled with spiritual wisdom provides a legacy that extends far beyond her own lifetime.

Men must recognize and support their wife's role as a nurturer, leader, and spiritual guide. A godly woman who feels empowered and valued by her husband will embrace her role wholeheartedly, leading to a household that flourishes in love and faith.

Why Embracing Her Wisdom Makes You a Better Leader

One of the greatest mistakes a man can make is overlooking the wisdom and insight of the woman God has placed in his life. A wise man understands that his wife's perspective is a blessing, not a challenge.

1. A Wise Man Honors and Embraces a Woman's Influence

The strongest leaders are those who value and respect the strengths of those around them. A husband who listens to his wife, considers her insights, and supports her growth fosters a relationship built on trust and mutual respect. He does not seek to suppress her influence but instead amplifies it, knowing that her wisdom is an asset to their shared journey.

Ephesians 5:25 calls men to *"love your wives, just as Christ loved the church and gave Himself up for her."* Just as Christ leads with sacrificial love, so too should a man lead in his marriage—honoring his wife's thoughts, ideas, and discernment.

2. Women Have Discernment and Intuition That Men Sometimes Overlook

Women possess a natural sense of intuition and discernment that allows them to perceive things men may not immediately recognize. Their emotional intelligence, spiritual sensitivity, and ability to foresee potential challenges make them invaluable partners in decision-making.

Many biblical women were instrumental in guiding their husbands toward wise choices. Abigail, in *1 Samuel 25:18-35*, used her wisdom to prevent David from making a rash decision that could have led to bloodshed. Her discernment saved her household and honored God's will. Similarly, Esther's bravery and strategic thinking saved the Jewish people from destruction (*Esther 4:14-16*).

A man who disregards his wife's wisdom misses out on one of the greatest sources of insight and support that God has given him. By embracing and valuing her perspective, he strengthens his leadership and enhances his ability to make sound decisions.

3. A Partnership Built on Mutual Respect Leads to Success

The most successful marriages and households are those where husband and wife work together in unity. A strong leader does not lead alone—he recognizes the value of partnership and collaboration.

When a man values his wife's wisdom, it strengthens their bond and allows their relationship to thrive. A husband who fosters an environment where his wife feels heard and valued will find that she pours even more love, encouragement, and wisdom into their relationship.

Colossians 3:19 reminds men: *"Husbands, love your wives and do not be harsh with them."* A man who leads with love and embraces his wife's influence will experience deeper connection, harmony, and spiritual growth in his household.

Final Thoughts

A woman's influence is one of the most powerful forces in a home. *Proverbs 14:1* teaches us that a wise woman builds up her household, shaping the lives of those around her with love, wisdom, and faith. However, for her influence to flourish, she must feel supported, valued, and cherished by her husband.

Men who foster love and respect in their homes create an environment where their wife's gifts can shine. By embracing her role as a nurturer, spiritual guide, and leader, a husband strengthens his own leadership and creates a legacy of faith and unity.

A wise man does not silence his wife—he listens to her, learns from her, and honors the wisdom that God has placed within her. By doing so, he builds a strong, God-centered home that reflects love, partnership, and divine purpose.

Chapter 6:
Handling Conflict in Marriage

Ephesians 4:26 – "Do Not Let the Sun Go Down on Your Anger"

Conflict is an inevitable part of any marriage, but how a couple handles conflict determines the strength and longevity of their relationship. *Ephesians 4:26* states: *"Do not let the sun go down on your anger."* This verse emphasizes the importance of addressing disputes quickly rather than allowing resentment to fester.

Unresolved conflict creates emotional distance and erodes trust. When disagreements arise, men must prioritize resolution over pride. Many marriages suffer not because of the presence of conflict but because of the inability to resolve it in a healthy and godly manner.

A husband who leads with wisdom and humility will recognize that peace in his marriage is more valuable than being "right." Conflict handled with love strengthens a relationship, while unresolved anger weakens it.

Why Unresolved Conflict Destroys Relationships

Many couples believe that avoiding arguments will maintain peace, but suppressed emotions don't disappear—they build up and explode later. Ignored conflicts turn into bitterness, silent resentment, and emotional distance.

Just as a neglected wound can become infected, unresolved conflict festers until it causes greater harm. Addressing issues early with humility and wisdom leads to lasting peace.

1. Unresolved Conflict Builds Emotional Walls

When a couple does not address their disagreements, emotional barriers begin to form. These walls create disconnect, misunderstanding, and coldness in the relationship. Over time, even small disagreements can feel overwhelming because past wounds remain unhealed.

Proverbs 17:14 says: *"Starting a quarrel is like breaching a dam; so drop the matter before a dispute breaks out."* Learning to address issues promptly prevents bigger problems from arising.

2. Suppressed Emotions Lead to Explosive Reactions

A person can only suppress hurt, frustration, and disappointment for so long before those emotions surface. When conflicts are ignored, they will manifest in passive-aggressive behavior, emotional withdrawal, or sudden outbursts of anger.

The Bible warns against the dangers of unresolved anger. *James 1:19-20* states: *"Everyone should be quick to listen, slow to speak and slow to become angry, because human anger does not produce the righteousness that God desires."* Handling conflict with patience and wisdom prevents destructive emotional reactions.

3. Avoiding Conflict Destroys Trust

Ignoring disagreements may seem like the easier path, but over time, avoidance erodes trust. A wife who feels that her concerns are constantly dismissed will eventually stop sharing her heart with her husband. This lack of communication weakens the foundation of the marriage.

A godly man understands that true leadership means creating a safe space where his wife's concerns are valued. Facing conflict with maturity and love deepens trust and strengthens the marriage bond.

How to Approach Disagreements with Wisdom and Grace

Conflict does not have to be destructive. When handled properly, disagreements can lead to growth, deeper understanding, and greater intimacy between a husband and wife.

1. Stay Calm – Raising Your Voice Escalates Conflict

A heated argument often leads to regretful words and unnecessary hurt. Staying calm during disagreements allows both partners to express themselves without fear of attack.

Proverbs 15:1 teaches: *"A gentle answer turns away wrath, but a harsh word stirs up anger."* Responding with gentleness rather than frustration can prevent conflicts from escalating.

If emotions start to rise, take a deep breath and pray for wisdom before continuing the discussion. Walking away for a brief moment to gather your thoughts can be more productive than engaging in an argument fueled by frustration.

2. Listen First – Let Her Speak Without Interruption

One of the most important elements of conflict resolution is **active listening.** Many men listen only to respond, rather than listening to understand. A woman desires to be heard and validated.

Proverbs 18:13 warns: *"To answer before listening—that is folly and shame."* Cutting off a conversation before truly hearing your wife's heart leads to frustration and unresolved pain.

Let your wife share her concerns without interrupting or jumping to conclusions. Sometimes, she simply needs to express her emotions without an immediate solution.

3. Find Solutions Together – Marriage is a Partnership, Not a Competition

Some men treat disagreements like battles to be won, but marriage is not about winning arguments—it is about **finding unity.** Instead of trying to be "right," a husband should seek a solution that benefits both partners.

Ecclesiastes 4:9 states: *"Two are better than one, because they have a good return for their labor."* A godly marriage thrives when both husband and wife work together to resolve conflicts with love and compromise.

4. Apologize and Forgive Quickly

No one is perfect, and every husband will make mistakes. A wise man is quick to apologize and ask for forgiveness when he is wrong. Similarly, a loving wife should be quick to forgive.

Colossians 3:13 teaches: *"Bear with each other and forgive one another if any of you has a grievance against someone. Forgive as the Lord forgave you."* A healthy marriage is built on grace, humility, and a willingness to move forward.

5. Pray Together After a Disagreement

A couple that prays together, stays together. Bringing God into conflict resolution creates an atmosphere of peace, healing, and restoration.

Philippians 4:6-7 encourages believers: *"Do not be anxious about anything, but in every situation, by prayer and petition, with thanksgiving, present your requests to God. And the peace of God, which transcends all understanding, will guard your hearts and your minds in Christ Jesus."*

When a husband and wife seek God's wisdom together, they invite His presence into their marriage. Praying after an argument helps realign hearts, fosters forgiveness, and reinforces the commitment to love each other as Christ loves the Church.

Final Thoughts

Handling conflict in marriage is about more than just avoiding fights—it is about building a foundation of trust, respect, and open communication. Ephesians 4:26 teaches that unresolved anger should not be carried into the next day. Addressing conflict promptly with love and wisdom prevents bitterness from taking root.

A husband who leads with humility, patience, and a listening heart creates an atmosphere where his wife feels valued and secure. Disagreements are inevitable, but when a couple commits to handling conflict with grace and biblical principles, their marriage will grow stronger, healthier, and more deeply rooted in love.

Let every husband ask himself: *Am I prioritizing resolution over pride? Am I listening with patience and understanding? Am I leading with love even in moments of conflict?* A godly man builds his marriage through compassion, wisdom, and a commitment to unity.

Chapter 7:
Understanding a Woman's Seasons in Life

Ecclesiastes 3:1 – "To Everything, There is a Season."

Life is constantly changing, and just as the seasons shift in nature, so do the seasons of a woman's life. *Ecclesiastes 3:1* reminds us: *"To everything, there is a season, and a time for every purpose under heaven."* Women go through various emotional, spiritual, and physical transitions throughout their lives, and a wise man must be patient and adaptable.

Understanding these seasons helps a husband support his wife with wisdom and love. A woman's needs will evolve as she journeys through life, and a man who embraces these changes with grace will build a strong, lasting relationship. Commitment remains steady, even as seasons shift.

How Women's Emotional and Spiritual Needs Change Over Time

Each stage of a woman's life brings new experiences, challenges, and desires. The key to a fulfilling marriage is recognizing these shifts and responding with understanding and encouragement.

1. Young Adulthood: She Seeks Affirmation and Purpose

During early adulthood, a woman is discovering her identity, aspirations, and place in the world. She desires affirmation, encouragement, and a strong emotional foundation to support her growth.

Proverbs 3:5-6 encourages trust in God's plan: *"Trust in the Lord with all your heart and lean not on your own understanding; in all your ways submit to Him, and He will make your paths straight."* A man should remind his wife or partner that she is deeply valued, both by him and by God.

A husband can support his wife in this season by:

- Encouraging her to pursue her dreams and God-given calling.
- Providing emotional security as she navigates career and life decisions.
- Speaking words of affirmation to strengthen her confidence.

2. Motherhood: She Needs Support, Patience, and Encouragement

Motherhood is a season of great joy and immense responsibility. Whether through childbirth, adoption, or caregiving, this stage is emotionally, physically, and spiritually demanding. Many women feel overwhelmed as they balance nurturing their children, maintaining their identity, and strengthening their marriage.

Isaiah 40:11 provides a comforting image: *"He tends His flock like a shepherd: He gathers the lambs in His arms and carries them close to His heart; He gently leads those that have young."* Just as God tenderly cares for mothers, husbands should do the same.

A husband can support his wife in this season by:

- Offering help and reassurance—simple acts of service like changing diapers, preparing meals, or giving her rest make a difference.
- Speaking words of encouragement—reminding her that she is an amazing mother and wife.
- Being present—quality time strengthens emotional intimacy, even amid busy schedules.

3. Middle Age: She Craves Deep Emotional Connection and Appreciation

As children grow and responsibilities shift, women begin to reflect on their life's journey. This is often a season of reevaluating priorities, rediscovering passions, and longing for deeper connection. If neglected, this stage can lead to loneliness or emotional discontent.

Proverbs 31:10 says: *"A wife of noble character who can find? She is worth far more than rubies."* A woman in this stage desires to know that her worth is recognized and her contributions appreciated.

A husband can support his wife in this season by:

- Reaffirming his love and appreciation verbally and through actions.
- Encouraging her to pursue personal goals and spiritual growth.
- Making an effort to rekindle romance and connection.

4. Senior Years: She Desires Companionship, Legacy, and Spiritual Depth

Later in life, women value companionship, reflection, and legacy. As the pace of life slows, relationships and spiritual fulfillment become a greater priority. This season is about cherishing memories, mentoring the next generation, and strengthening faith.

Titus 2:3-5 speaks of older women mentoring younger women, demonstrating the importance of passing on wisdom. A wife at this stage wants to know that her life has made a meaningful impact.

A husband can support **his wife in this season by:**

- Spending quality time reflecting on shared memories and faith.
- Encouraging her to pour into others—through ministry, mentoring, or family involvement.
- Deepening their spiritual journey together through prayer and study.

How to Support Her Through Life's Transitions

Seasons change, but commitment remains. A man who embraces the shifts in his wife's journey will build a strong, enduring marriage founded on love, patience, and faith.

1. Be Understanding and Adaptable

Women's needs, emotions, and perspectives will evolve over time. A husband who recognizes these shifts and adapts accordingly creates an environment of trust and security.

1 Peter 3:7 teaches: *"Husbands, in the same way, be considerate as you live with your wives, and treat them with respect as the weaker partner and as heirs with you of the gracious gift of life, so that nothing will hinder your prayers."* Consideration and adaptability strengthen marriage.

A husband can practice adaptability by:

- Adjusting his expectations as his wife's responsibilities and needs change.
- Being patient and supportive when she experiences emotional or spiritual growth.
- Providing reassurance that his love is constant, no matter the season.

2. Encourage Her Growth

A husband should celebrate his wife's evolving interests, passions, and personal growth. Supporting her dreams and spiritual walk reinforces that she is deeply valued.

Philippians 1:6 reminds us: *"Being confident of this, that He who began a good work in you will carry it on to completion until the day of Christ Jesus."* God continues to work in every season, and a husband should encourage his wife's journey.

Practical ways to encourage her growth:

- Support her in pursuing new goals, studies, or hobbies.
- Pray for her and with her as she deepens her spiritual journey.
- Be her biggest encourager, especially when she faces self-doubt.

3. Provide Reassurance – Women Need to Feel Secure and Valued

In every stage of life, a woman needs to feel safe, cherished, and valued. She must know that her husband sees her as a blessing, not a burden.

Isaiah 41:10 says: "Do not fear, for I am with you; do not be dismayed, for I am your God. I will strengthen you and help you; I will uphold you with my righteous right hand." Just as God reassures His people, a husband should provide comfort and security to his wife.

Ways to provide reassurance:

- Speak life-giving words—regularly remind her that she is loved and appreciated.
- Be present—spend time together without distractions.
- Honor your commitment—demonstrate that your love is steadfast through every season.

Final Thoughts

Marriage is a lifelong journey through seasons of joy, change, challenge, and growth. A husband who understands and embraces his wife's evolving emotional and spiritual needs builds a foundation of love, trust, and unity.

By practicing patience, encouraging growth, and providing steadfast reassurance, a man strengthens his marriage and honors God's design for relationships.

Let every husband ask himself: *Am I walking beside my wife in every season? Am I providing the support and love she needs? Am I leading our marriage with wisdom and grace?* A godly man loves his wife through every transition, just as Christ loves His Church—faithfully, sacrificially, and with unwavering devotion.

Chapter 8:
The Woman as a Life-Giver and Enhancer

Titus 2:4-5 – Women Are Designed to Nurture and Uplift

Women are created with an innate ability to nurture, uplift, and breathe life into those around them. Titus 2:4-5 calls for women to be loving, kind, and dedicated to their families, illustrating their crucial role in creating warmth and stability within a home.

A woman is a natural caregiver, providing emotional, spiritual, and physical nourishment to her family and community. Her ability to encourage, support, and strengthen those around her is a divine gift. A man's role is to recognize, honor, and support this gift, rather than take it for granted.

When a woman feels valued and appreciated, she flourishes and, in turn, multiplies love, peace, and stability in her household. A wise husband understands that his support and encouragement help his wife become the best version of herself.

The Power of Encouragement and Emotional Support

A woman thrives when she feels emotionally supported and uplifted. Her confidence and ability to nurture those around her are strengthened when she knows she is deeply loved and appreciated.

1. Simple Words of Affirmation Go a Long Way

Words have power. A woman who hears **consistent encouragement and appreciation** from her husband will feel secure and confident in her role. Too often, husbands assume their wives know they are loved and appreciated, yet **affirmation must be spoken and demonstrated regularly.**

Proverbs 16:24 says: "Gracious words are a honeycomb, sweet to the soul and healing to the bones." Words of affirmation can heal, uplift, and bring joy.

Examples of affirming words:

- *"I appreciate everything you do for our family."*
- *"You are an incredible wife and mother."*
- *"Your kindness and strength inspire me every day."*

These simple expressions strengthen emotional security, making a woman feel seen and valued.

2. A Woman Thrives When She Feels Emotionally Supported

Emotional support means being present, attentive, and engaged. Women carry significant emotional and mental loads—balancing responsibilities, relationships, and spiritual well-being. A husband who provides emotional support helps relieve that weight and strengthens their bond.

Ecclesiastes 4:9-10 reminds us: *"Two are better than one... If either of them falls down, one can help the other up."* A strong marriage is built on mutual encouragement and partnership.

Ways to offer emotional support:

- **Listen attentively**—sometimes she just needs to talk and feel heard.
- **Offer reassurance**—remind her she's doing an amazing job.

- **Be patient and understanding**—acknowledge her emotions and struggles.

A woman who feels emotionally supported is more likely to be joyful, secure, and empowered in all aspects of life.

How Men Can Empower the Women in Their Lives to Flourish

A wise man does not limit or suppress his wife—he empowers her to grow, thrive, and reach her full potential. Encouraging a woman's spiritual, emotional, and personal growth is one of the greatest expressions of love and respect.

1. Give Her Space to Grow Spiritually, Mentally, and Emotionally

Women are constantly evolving, just as men are. A husband who encourages his wife's spiritual, emotional, and intellectual growth fosters a relationship filled with mutual respect and admiration.

Philippians 1:6 says: *"Being confident of this, that He who began a good work in you will carry it on to completion until the day of Christ Jesus."* Just as God continues to work in each of us, a husband should celebrate his wife's journey of **growth and transformation.**

Ways to encourage her growth:

- Support her in studying Scripture and deepening her faith.
- Encourage her to pursue her passions, education, or career.
- Give her time for self-care, reflection, and renewal.

A husband who nurtures his wife's spiritual and emotional well-being strengthens not only her but also their marriage and family.

2. Celebrate Her Strengths and Contributions

A woman's contributions to her home, family, and community are immeasurable. Whether she is a mother, wife, professional, caregiver, or leader, her role is significant. A man should recognize, appreciate, and celebrate her efforts regularly.

Proverbs 31:28 states: "Her children arise and call her blessed; her husband also, and he praises her." A godly man understands that his wife's value is far greater than rubies.

Ways to celebrate her strengths:

- Publicly and privately acknowledge her efforts.
- Offer help and support rather than expecting her to manage everything alone.
- Encourage her dreams, goals, and ambitions.

A woman who is celebrated and appreciated is more likely to be fulfilled, joyful, and empowered in her role as a wife, mother, and spiritual leader.

Final Thoughts

Women are life-givers, nurturers, and enhancers. A wise man understands that his role is not to suppress or control his wife but to uplift, support, and empower her so that she flourishes in her God-given purpose.

Ephesians 5:25 teaches: *"Husbands, love your wives, just as Christ loved the church and gave Himself up for her."* Jesus's love was sacrificial, empowering, and nurturing—the same type of love a husband should demonstrate to his wife.

By offering words of affirmation, emotional support, and encouragement for growth, a man helps his wife become all that God has called her to be. In turn, she will multiply love, peace, and wisdom within their home, relationship, and beyond.

Let every husband ask himself: *Am I encouraging my wife daily? Am I creating an environment where she feels valued and supported? Am I celebrating her as a life-giver and enhancer?* A godly man recognizes and nurtures the gift that a woman is, ensuring she shines in her full potential, for the glory of God and the strength of their marriage.

Chapter 9:
The Importance of Spiritual Leadership

Ephesians 5:23 – Men Are Called to Be Spiritual Leaders

The role of a man in a relationship extends beyond provision and protection—he is called to be the spiritual leader of his home. *Ephesians 5:23* states: *"For the husband is the head of the wife, as Christ is the head of the church, his body, of which He is the Savior."* This verse does not call for domination or control but for godly leadership rooted in love, sacrifice, and faithfulness.

A man's spiritual leadership is not about authority but responsibility. His relationship with God sets the tone for his household. When a man prioritizes his spiritual growth, his wife and children benefit from his guidance and wisdom.

A true leader leads by example, not by force. He encourages his family to walk in faith through his actions, words, and dedication to God. A husband who seeks God with all his heart creates a foundation of faith that strengthens his marriage and household.

How a Man's Faith Impacts His Wife and Family

The strength of a man's spiritual walk directly influences his wife's emotional and spiritual well-being. His faith acts as a covering of protection, guidance, and encouragement.

1. When a Man Prays, Seeks Wisdom, and Leads in Faith, His Family Follows

A spiritually grounded man sets an example of godliness in his home. His commitment to prayer, Scripture, and integrity encourages his wife and children to seek God as well.

Proverbs 20:7 says: *"The righteous man walks in his integrity; his children are blessed after him."* A man who walks in faith creates a legacy of righteousness that impacts future generations.

Practical ways to lead spiritually:

- **Pray daily**—for wisdom, strength, and for your family's needs.
- **Study Scripture**—seeking biblical guidance for decisions.
- **Live with integrity**—so that your actions reflect Christ's love.

2. Spiritual Leadership Isn't About Control—It's About Serving with Love

Many misunderstand spiritual leadership as dominance, but true leadership is servant-hearted. Jesus led His disciples through humility, sacrifice, and love—this is how a man should lead his wife.

Mark 10:45 states: *"For even the Son of Man did not come to be served, but to serve, and to give His life as a ransom for many."* A husband leads by serving, putting his wife's well-being above his own.

Ways to serve in spiritual leadership:

- **Encourage her faith**—support her spiritual walk and prayer life.

- **Be patient and understanding**—as she grows in her own journey with God.
- **Lead without arrogance**—seek God's wisdom rather than acting on pride.

A man's gentle and loving leadership fosters peace, trust, and spiritual growth in his household.

Building a Home That Honors God

A home that honors God is built on a foundation of faith, prayer, and biblical values. A spiritually strong man leads his family toward godly principles, moral integrity, and unwavering faith.

1. Prioritize Prayer, Church, and Spiritual Discussions

A husband who prioritizes spiritual practices strengthens his marriage and provides a firm foundation for his children. Faith must be cultivated intentionally, not left to chance.

Joshua 24:15 proclaims: *"As for me and my household, we will serve the Lord."* A man must declare this same commitment for his home.

Ways to create a God-honoring home:

- **Pray as a family**—before meals, bedtime, and during struggles.
- **Attend church together**—building a strong faith community.
- **Discuss Scripture**—helping each other grow in biblical wisdom.

When faith is at the center, the home becomes a place of peace, love, and spiritual growth.

2. Set Biblical Values in Your Home

Every household operates by a set of values—these should be rooted in God's Word. A husband must lead in establishing and upholding biblical principles within the family.

Psalm 127:1 says: *"Unless the Lord builds the house, the builders labor in vain."* Without God's presence, a home is spiritually vulnerable.

Key biblical values to establish:

- **Love and Respect** (*Ephesians 5:33*)—treating each other with Christlike love.
- **Integrity and Honesty** (*Proverbs 11:3*)—modeling godly character.
- **Forgiveness and Grace** (*Colossians 3:13*)—practicing mercy and understanding.

By upholding these values, a man builds a home that reflects Christ's love and truth.

Final Thoughts

A man's spiritual leadership is one of his greatest responsibilities in marriage. *Ephesians 5:23* calls men to lead with wisdom, love, and faith. This role is not about control but about guiding his family toward Christ.

By prioritizing prayer, seeking wisdom, and leading with humility, a man creates a household that honors God and thrives spiritually.

Let every husband ask himself: *Am I leading my family toward Christ? Am I setting a spiritual example in my home? Am I serving with love and humility?* A godly man builds his house on faith, ensuring that his wife and children walk in God's truth and grace.

Chapter 10: Honoring and Protecting Women

A Man's Duty to Honor and Protect

Honoring a woman is not just about words of appreciation; it is about consistent actions that show she is valued, respected, and cherished. *1 Peter 3:7* teaches men: *"Husbands, likewise, dwell with them with understanding, giving honor to the wife as to the weaker vessel, and as being heirs together of the grace of life, that your prayers may not be hindered."*

This scripture highlights three key responsibilities for men:

1. **Understanding** – A man must seek to understand a woman's emotions, thoughts, and needs.
2. **Honor** – He must treat her with deep respect and dignity.
3. **Protection** – He must safeguard her emotionally, physically, and spiritually.

A man who follows these principles not only strengthens his relationship with his wife but also reflects godly character and leadership. Honoring and protecting a woman is a reflection of his integrity, love, and commitment to Christ.

How to Honor Women in Everyday Life

Honoring a woman is not about grand gestures alone; it is about daily acts of love and respect that affirm her worth and importance in the relationship.

1. Respect Her Words & Feelings

A woman desires to be heard, not dismissed. Many conflicts in relationships arise because men fail to listen actively. A wise man does not merely hear his wife—he listens with his heart, not just his ears.

Proverbs 18:13 warns: *"To answer before listening—that is folly and shame."* Taking the time to understand a woman's feelings and perspectives strengthens the emotional bond in a marriage.

Ways to show respect:

- **Listen attentively**—do not interrupt or dismiss her concerns.
- **Acknowledge her emotions**—validate her feelings rather than belittling them.
- **Respond with patience and kindness**—a gentle answer turns away conflict (*Proverbs 15:1*).

2. Encourage & Uplift Her

A woman thrives when she feels supported and encouraged. Simple words of affirmation can strengthen her confidence and bring her peace.

Proverbs 16:24 says: *"Gracious words are a honeycomb, sweet to the soul and healing to the bones."* Words have the power to either build up or break down a woman's spirit.

Encouraging words to say daily:

- *"I appreciate everything you do for our family."*
- *"You are strong, beautiful, and loved."*
- *"Your kindness and wisdom inspire me."*

When a man consistently uplifts his wife, he creates an environment where she flourishes emotionally and spiritually.

3. Lead with Integrity

A man who is consistent in his words and actions builds trust and security in a woman's heart. Honoring a woman means leading with honesty, faithfulness, and dependability.

Proverbs 10:9 says: *"Whoever walks in integrity walks securely, but whoever takes crooked paths will be found out."* A man of integrity does not say one thing and do another—his actions align with his words.

Ways to lead with integrity:

- **Be faithful and honest**—trust is built through consistency.
- **Make wise, God-honoring decisions**—seek biblical guidance.
- **Take responsibility**—admit mistakes and work to improve.

A woman feels secure when she knows her husband walks in truth, faith, and moral integrity.

How to Protect Women

Protecting a woman is not about control; it is about ensuring her safety, well-being, and emotional peace.

1. Protect Her Physically

A man's duty is to protect his wife from harm and danger. This includes being a source of strength, ensuring safety, and never being a source of fear or violence.

Psalm 82:3-4 commands: *"Defend the weak and the fatherless; uphold the cause of the poor and the oppressed. Rescue the weak and the needy."*

How to protect her physically:

- **Ensure her safety**—whether at home, in public, or while traveling.
- **Never raise a hand in anger**—abuse is completely against God's design.
- **Stand up for her**—if someone disrespects or threatens her, defend her with wisdom and strength.

2. Protect Her Emotionally

A woman is deeply affected by how she is treated. Emotional wounds last longer than physical ones, and neglect, sarcasm, or harsh words can cause deep pain.

Colossians 3:19 warns: *"Husbands, love your wives and do not be harsh with them."* Love should be gentle, kind, and nurturing.

Ways to protect her emotions:

- Avoid sarcasm, insults, and dismissiveness—words have lasting impact.
- Be her safe place—let her express herself without fear of judgment.
- Reassure her of your love and commitment—affirm her value regularly.

3. Protect Her Spiritually

A man's faith impacts his wife. When a husband is spiritually strong, he covers his wife in prayer, encouragement, and godly leadership.

Ephesians 6:18 reminds us to *"pray in the Spirit on all occasions with all kinds of prayers and requests."* A husband should pray for, with, and over his wife daily.

Ways to provide spiritual protection:

- Pray with her and for her—bring her concerns before God.
- Encourage her faith—support her spiritual growth.
- Live as a godly example—model faithfulness in action.

A woman who feels spiritually protected thrives in her faith, confidence, and emotional well-being.

Final Thoughts

The way a man honors and protects a woman reflects his character, integrity, and love for God. A man who treats his wife with kindness, respect, and selflessness creates a stronger relationship, deeper connection, and lasting peace in his home.

Ephesians 5:25 reminds us: *"Husbands, love your wives, just as Christ loved the church and gave Himself up for her."* Jesus's love was sacrificial, nurturing, and protective—this is how a husband should love his wife.

Let every man ask himself: *Am I honoring my wife daily? Am I protecting her physically, emotionally, and spiritually? Am I leading our marriage with Christlike love?* A godly man builds his relationship on respect, encouragement, and unwavering protection, ensuring his wife feels valued and cherished in every aspect of life.

Chapter 11:
The Woman as a Reflector

Women Mirror What They Receive

A woman reflects what is poured into her. *Proverbs 27:19* says: *"As in water face reflects face, so the heart of man reflects man."* Just as water reflects an image, a woman reflects the love, kindness, and care that she receives from her husband.

If a man pours love, security, and affirmation into a woman, she will reflect joy, peace, and gratitude. However, if he pours neglect, anger, and criticism, she will reflect pain, frustration, and withdrawal.

The way a man treats his wife will be mirrored back in their relationship. A wise man understands that his actions, words, and attitudes set the tone for his home.

How a Woman Responds to a Man's Leadership

A woman does not merely respond to words—she responds to consistent actions and emotional investment. Her behavior in a relationship is often a reflection of how she is treated.

1. If You Encourage Her, She Will Thrive

A woman who feels appreciated and valued will go above and beyond to build a strong and joyful relationship. Encouragement strengthens her confidence and deepens her emotional connection with her husband.

Proverbs 31:28 says: *"Her children arise and call her blessed; her husband also, and he praises her."* A woman who is praised and uplifted flourishes in her marriage and family.

How to encourage her:

- Acknowledge her efforts—thank her for all she does, both big and small.
- Support her dreams—encourage her in her passions and goals.
- Express gratitude daily—simple words like "I appreciate you" have lasting impact.

2. If You Dismiss Her, She Will Shut Down

A woman who feels ignored, dismissed, or belittled will eventually close her heart. If a man is emotionally distant or cold, she will stop opening up and withdraw from the relationship.

Ephesians 4:29 warns: *"Do not let any unwholesome talk come out of your mouths, but only what is helpful for building others up according to their needs."* Words that belittle or dismiss a woman's emotions cause emotional distance in the marriage.

Signs she is shutting down:

- She stops sharing her thoughts and feelings.
- She becomes emotionally distant or quiet.
- She no longer seeks connection or reassurance from her husband.

How to prevent emotional shutdown:

- Listen without interruption—give her space to express her heart.
- Validate her feelings—acknowledge her emotions rather than dismiss them.

- Be attentive—small acts of love show that she is heard and valued.

3. If You Protect Her, She Will Trust You

When a woman feels physically, emotionally, and spiritually safe, she becomes more secure and confident in the relationship. Protection does not just mean physical safety—it means being a safe place for her emotions, thoughts, and spirit.

Proverbs 18:10 says: *"The name of the Lord is a fortified tower; the righteous run to it and are safe."* Just as God is a refuge, a man should be a refuge of safety and security for his wife.

Ways to create a sense of security:

- **Be consistent in your actions**—trust is built through reliability.
- **Defend her honor**—never allow others to speak poorly of her.
- **Pray over her and with her**—covering her in prayer fosters emotional and spiritual security.

Practical Ways to Lead with Love

A man's role as a leader is **not about control—it is about love, consistency, and strength.** When a man leads with love, his wife will naturally reflect that love back into the relationship.

1. Speak to Her Gently, Even in Frustration

A man's tone of voice and choice of words greatly impact his wife's emotional well-being. Even in disagreements, speaking with gentleness maintains trust and respect.

Proverbs 15:1 says: *"A gentle answer turns away wrath, but a harsh word stirs up anger."*

How to practice gentle communication:

- Pause before responding—avoid speaking in frustration.
- Use words that build up—affirm rather than tear down.
- Control your emotions—respond with patience and wisdom.

2. Encourage Her Dreams and Passions

A woman needs support and encouragement to grow spiritually, emotionally, and mentally. A husband who nurtures her growth strengthens the marriage.

Philippians 2:4 says: *"Let each of you look not only to his own interests, but also to the interests of others."* Supporting a woman's goals and aspirations fosters unity and fulfillment.

Ways to encourage her growth:

- Ask about her dreams and goals.
- Celebrate her achievements, no matter how small.
- Provide time and space for her personal development.

3. Be the Emotional and Spiritual Leader in Your Home

A man's faith and emotional stability set the tone for the marriage. If he is rooted in Christ, he provides a foundation of security for his wife.

Ephesians 5:23 teaches: *"For the husband is the head of the wife, as Christ is the head of the church, his body, of which he is the Savior."* A husband is called to lead with wisdom, love, and selflessness.

Ways to lead spiritually and emotionally:

- Initiate prayer together—cover your marriage in faith.
- Set an example of godly character—live with integrity.
- Be present and engaged—show consistent emotional support.

4. Show Consistency—Don't Let Your Mood Dictate How You Treat Her

A woman's security in a relationship is deeply tied to consistency. If a man is unpredictable or moody, she will feel uneasy and uncertain. Emotional stability builds trust.

James 1:19 advises: *"Everyone should be quick to listen, slow to speak and slow to become angry."* A man who controls his emotions fosters peace and safety in his home.

How to demonstrate consistency:

- Stay kind and patient, even during stressful times.
- Keep your promises—follow through on commitments.
- Show affection daily—love should not be conditional.

Final Thoughts

A woman reflects what is poured into her. A loved, cherished, and supported woman will multiply that love and joy back into the marriage. Conversely, a neglected or unappreciated woman will struggle to give what she does not receive.

Ephesians 5:25 reminds husbands: *"Love your wives, just as Christ loved the church and gave Himself up for her."* Jesus sacrificially loved, nurtured, and uplifted the church—this is the model of true biblical leadership.

Let every man ask himself: *What is my wife reflecting back to me? Am I leading with love and encouragement? Am I creating an environment where she thrives?* A man who pours love, patience, and wisdom into his wife will see that same love reflected back in a joyful, peaceful home.

Chapter 12:
The Ultimate Call – Loving Your Wife as Christ Loved the Church

The Highest Standard of Love

The Bible commands husbands:

"Husbands, love your wives, just as Christ also loved the church and gave Himself for her." (*Ephesians 5:25*)

This is not just a suggestion—it is a command. Christ's love for the Church serves as the ultimate standard for how a husband should love his wife.

Christ's love was:

1. **Sacrificial** – He gave His life for His people. A man must give his time, energy, and love to his wife, prioritizing her well-being over personal convenience.

2. **Unconditional** – He loves us despite our flaws. A man must love his wife in all circumstances, not just when it is easy or when she meets expectations.

3. **Faithful** – Christ never abandons His people. A man must remain devoted and loyal to his wife, cherishing her throughout life's trials and triumphs.

A marriage built on Christ-like love will be strong, fulfilling, and enduring. When a husband mirrors Christ's selfless love, he fosters a home of peace, trust, and joy.

What Does It Mean to Love Like Christ?

Loving as Christ loved the Church requires more than affection—it requires selflessness, patience, and leadership. A godly husband prioritizes his wife's needs above his own and creates an environment of safety, grace, and unwavering love.

1. Put Her Needs Before Your Own

Love is about giving, not just receiving. True leadership means prioritizing your wife's well-being, supporting her spiritually, emotionally, and physically.

Philippians 2:3-4 states: *"Do nothing out of selfish ambition or vain conceit. Rather, in humility value others above yourselves, not looking to your own interests but each of you to the interests of the others."*

Ways to put her needs first:

- Be attentive to her struggles—listen, encourage, and support her.
- Show acts of service—help with daily responsibilities without being asked.
- Make quality time a priority—your presence and attention strengthen your bond.

2. Be Patient and Forgiving

No marriage is perfect. Challenges will arise, and mistakes will be made. A grace-filled husband fosters peace, choosing patience over frustration and forgiveness over resentment.

Colossians 3:13 commands: *"Bear with each other and forgive one another if any of you has a grievance against someone. Forgive as the Lord forgave you."*

How to practice patience and forgiveness:

- Respond with grace, not anger—harsh words damage trust.
- Give second chances—just as Christ forgives, extend mercy.
- Let go of past hurts—do not hold grudges or bring up old conflicts.

3. Protect Her Heart

A husband must guard his wife's heart from emotional harm, ensuring that pride, anger, and selfishness do not damage their bond.

Proverbs 4:23 advises: *"Above all else, guard your heart, for everything you do flows from it."*

Ways to protect her heart:

- Speak with kindness and affirmation.
- Be transparent and honest.
- Avoid emotional neglect—check in on her feelings and concerns.

Real-Life Examples of Christ-Like Love

The Bible provides powerful examples of men who demonstrated Christ-like love in their marriages. Their stories illustrate honor, commitment, and sacrificial love.

1. Boaz (Ruth 2-4) – Honored, Provided, and Cherished

Boaz showed kindness, integrity, and protection toward Ruth. He ensured her well-being, provided for her needs, and treated her with dignity and care.

Lessons from Boaz:

- Provide security—whether financially, emotionally, or spiritually.
- Honor your wife's worth—treat her with admiration and respect.
- Lead with compassion—love should be shown through action, not just words.

2. Joseph (Mary's Husband) – Protected, Honored, and Loved

Even when circumstances were uncertain, Joseph protected Mary from shame, honored their marriage, and trusted God's plan.

Lessons from Joseph:

- Stand by your wife in difficult times.
- Protect her reputation and dignity.
- Trust God's plan even when challenges arise.

3. Modern-Day Husbands – Loving, Serving, and Uplifting

Men who follow Christ's example in marriage experience stronger relationships, deeper intimacy, and lasting fulfillment. A selfless husband creates an environment where his wife feels safe, cherished, and empowered.

Practical Steps for Deepening Love in Marriage

Every husband can take intentional steps to cultivate a Christ-centered marriage.

1. Pray Together Daily

A couple that prays together builds a stronger spiritual connection. Inviting God into your marriage strengthens faith, unity, and love.

Matthew 18:20 says: *"For where two or three gather in my name, there am I with them."*

Ways to implement prayer:

- Start each morning by praying together.
- Pray over each other's burdens and dreams.
- Ask for God's wisdom in marriage.

2. Continue Dating Your Wife

Romance should never fade in marriage. Continue to date your wife, pursue her heart, and make her feel special.

Song of Solomon 4:7 expresses: *"You are altogether beautiful, my darling; there is no flaw in you."*

Ideas to keep love alive:

- Plan intentional date nights.
- Surprise her with small gestures of love.
- Express your affection daily.

3. Speak Life Into Her

A man's words shape the atmosphere of his home. Words can build up or tear down—choose life-giving words that encourage and strengthen.

Proverbs 18:21 says: *"The tongue has the power of life and death."*

How to speak life:

- Compliment her strengths and efforts.
- Encourage her when she feels discouraged.
- Remind her daily of her worth and beauty.

Final Thoughts

This book is not just about understanding women—it is about understanding love, leadership, and relationships through God's eyes.

A godly husband reflects Christ's love—sacrificial, patient, and unwavering. By leading with faith, loving with selflessness, and prioritizing his wife's well-being, a man creates a marriage that mirrors God's divine design.

If you want to build a stronger marriage, a healthier family, and a deeper connection with the women in your life, the answer is simple:

💡 Love as Christ loved.

www.ingramcontent.com/pod-product-compliance
Lightning Source LLC
LaVergne TN
LVHW052038080426
835513LV00018B/2380